Gloria ~

God ~

Margaret Weaver

Don't Give Up

Margaret Olivia Weaver

authorHOUSE®

AuthorHouse™
1663 Liberty Drive, Suite 200
Bloomington, IN 47403
www.authorhouse.com
Phone: 1-800-839-8640

First published by AuthorHouse 7/26/2010
ISBN: 978-1-4389-5442-4 (sc)

Unless otherwise indicated, all scripture references are from the King James Version of the Bible (KJV)

Scripture quotations marked "NIV" are taken from the HOLY BIBLE, NEW INTERNATIONAL VERSION®. NIV® Copyright ©1973, 1978, 1984 by International Bible Society. Used by permission of Zondervan. All rights reserved.

Scripture quotations marked "NKJV" are taken from the NEW KING JAMES VERSION®. Copyright © 1982 by Thomas Nelson, Inc. Used by permission. All rights reserved.

Scripture quotations marked "MSG" are taken from The Message. Copyright © 1993, 1994, 1995, 2000, 2001, 2002. Used by permission of NavPress Publishing Group.

Printed in the United States of America
This book is printed on acid-free paper.

Dedication

To my father, the late Dr. George Edward Weaver and my mother, Mrs. Mae Smith Weaver, God's precious gifts to me, I love you and I thank you.

Contents

Part II: Living And Learning

Acknowledgments

To God be the glory, the honor, and the praise. Great is Thy faithfulness! I would also like to express special thanks to:

My loving parents, George and Mae Weaver – for providing such a peaceful, joy-filled home. I am so grateful. It was an immeasurable blessing to hear your prayers. Your love and the sense of security I felt in our home made it easier for me to believe in a God who can be trusted.

Dr. Cameron and Mrs. Barbara Alexander, my pastor and his wife, and the Antioch church family – for the glorious privilege to be a part of a dynamic, life-changing ministry. God bless you Pastor Alexander for boldly and uncompromisingly preaching the gospel of Jesus Christ.

Pastor Charles Walker – for allowing God to use you many years ago in such a pivotal way in my life. Your love for God and His Word was contagious.

Pastors James and Sandra Lilly, friends for over 30 years, and prayer partner Deborah Cleveland – for literally decades of prayer support. How encouraging to know that daily your prayers are offered to God on my behalf.

Dr. Mack King and Patricia Carter and the New Mount Olive church family - for your prayers, kindness, and many expressions of love to the Weaver family.

Dr. David Hermecz and Dr. Joyce Webb – for the opportunity to have a 18-year (and counting) business partnership with two believers who love the Lord and seek His wisdom.

Pastor Frederick Robinson and my mother's dear friend Maude Humphries – for your editorial expertise. I so appreciate your assistance with this project.

John Thomas and Dr. Connie Ward – for your editorial comments, final review, and your friendship through the years.

Introduction

The title, *Don't Give Up*, is taken from Part I of the book, which emphasizes the importance of persevering when confronted with difficult challenges and painful life experiences. When faced with adversity, it is sometimes tempting to give up, quit, surrender to despair, and accept defeat. But, hopefully, you will be encouraged to keep pressing on during those tumultuous, and, at times, seemingly unrelenting storms of life.

Living And Learning, Part II of the book, focuses on other life lessons that teach us how to grow and trust God, His will, His way, and His Word.

Prayerfully, the book, in its entirety, will glorify God and give you hope, comfort, and inspirational thoughts for the journey.

Don't Give Up

Part I

Traveling Through A Storm

STORM LESSON (1)

Then they cried out to the Lord in their trouble, and he brought them out of their distress. He stilled the storm to a whisper; the waves of the sea were hushed. They were glad when it grew calm, and he guided them to their desired haven (Psalm 107:28-30 NIV).

Don't give up. Don't give up. Don't give up. Don't give in. Don't give out. Life has its ups and downs, its trials and tribulations, its troubles and struggles, its disappointments and disillusionments. There are times when it seems as if all the doors have been closed, all the options exhausted, all the opportunities thwarted, all the dreams deferred, and all the hope gone. But don't give up.

One day when I was a young driver, I found myself in a terrible storm. My father was in the passenger's seat and my mother was in the backseat. The lightning was flashing, the thunder was roaring, the rain pounded the car. It was not a very comfortable situation for a young, inexperienced driver. Cars were pulling off to the right and to the left. My mother thought it was best for me to pull over as well. So she asked my father, "George, don't you think it's time for Margaret to pull over?" He asked me, "Margaret, can you see?" I said, "Yes, Daddy I can see." He said, "Well, just keep going."

The storm did not get better; it got worse. I too thought it was time to pull over. But my father asked again, "Margaret, can you see?" I said, "Yes, Daddy I can see." He said, "Well, just keep going." I kept driving through a seemingly relentless storm. Then suddenly, the rain stopped, the thunder stopped, the lightning stopped. We were out of the storm. Initially, my father did not say a word, but after I drove for awhile, he asked me, "Margaret, do you remember those cars back there that pulled off to the side of the road?" "Yes," I replied. He said, "They are still in the storm."

What an unforgettable and invaluable lesson! When in the storms of life, do not pull over and stop. Keep going. In His time, God will speak "Peace be still" to the storms in your life. Don't give up!

Travel Lightly

STORM LESSON (2)

Then Elisha said, "Call her." So he called her, and she stood in the doorway. "About this time next year," Elisha said, "you will hold a son in your arms" (2 Kings 4:15-16 NIV).

The story is told of a woman who lived centuries ago who suffered a great, heartbreaking tragedy – the loss of a child. God promised her a son, and, true to His word, in a year's time she had a son. But later, he was suddenly stricken by an illness and died in her arms. She found herself in the midst of a horrendous storm. This woman, called

7

the Shunammite woman, decided to go to Mount Carmel and find Elisha, the prophet who promised her she would have the child. Her child was dead, but the promise was still alive.

When she approached her husband about her plans to go to Mount Carmel, she asked him for only two things: one donkey and one servant. Nothing more. Traveling even a short distance requires many women to load up with a lot of baggage. But this woman was in a hurry and in a storm. It's best to travel lightly in a storm.

Many find it difficult to make it through adversity because they are carrying too much baggage. Too many unresolved issues slow them down. The baggage of guilt weighs them down. The baggage of unforgiveness tears them down. The baggage of shame breaks them down. Through prayer, through wise counsel, through whatever means God provides, find a way to get rid of the baggage. It will slow you down, weigh you down, tear you down, and break you down.

The Shunammite woman was able to make her way to the prophet Elisha, and God used him as His instrument to bring the boy back to life. She held onto the promise even in her storm. And you can make it through yours. Just remember: travel lightly in a storm.

Shut The Door!

STORM LESSON (3)

The child grew, and one day he went out to his father, who was with the reapers. "My head! My head!" he said to his father. His father told a servant, "Carry him to his mother." After the servant had lifted him up and carried him to his mother, the boy sat on her lap until noon, and then he died. She went up and laid him on the bed of the man of God, then shut the door and went out (2 Kings 4:18-21 NIV).

When driving a car through turbulent, bad weather, it is reassuring to have someone else sharing the experience with you. The same is true of life's stormy weather. Knowing that others are with you, praying with you, believing with you, and standing with you, is reassuring and comforting. Indeed, *"A friend loves at all times, and a brother is born for adversity"* (Proverbs 17:17 NIV).

Yet during the boisterous winds of painful disappointments and trials, there are also times when it is necessary to retreat and commune with God – alone. Friends may continue to pray, but if we are to navigate our way through the storm, inevitably we must come face to face with our God. We will need His next step for our situation. When the Shunammite woman in 2 Kings 4 realized her son was dead, she put him in a room and "shut the door" literally and figuratively. She did not even tell her husband that their son was dead. Instead, this very determined mother made her way to the prophet Elisha who God used to miraculously restore life to her child.

Even Jesus, who obviously enjoyed the company of others, would steal away from the crowds and

His disciples to talk with His Father. While we should warmly receive the support, the prayers, the encouragement, and the comfort of our friends and family, remain sensitive to those inner urgings that prompt us to "shut the door" and allow the God who still calms storms to speak to the turbulence in our lives.

Divine Delays Are Not Denials

Being confident of this very thing, that he which hath begun a good work in you will perform it until the day of Jesus Christ (Philippians 1:6).

There is a scene from an old movie that is fascinating. Allied soldiers must destroy a dam to complete a mission. Three soldiers and a demolitions expert are assigned the task. Two of the men place the explosives in the dam while the demolitions expert and the other soldier remain some distance away. When the dynamite is set off, there is a small rumble, but, seemingly, the dam remains intact. The soldier begins to berate the demolitions expert and questions his competence, but the demolitions expert remains calm and does not appear disturbed. The man continues to yell, rant and rave. Still the demolitions expert is unfazed. After a period of time, noise begins to emanate from the dam. A crack begins to form. More noise. More cracks. Finally, the dam collapses, water pours out, a bridge collapses, and the mission is accomplished.

In our walk with the Lord, we may question life's delays and wonder why God is not moving fast enough. We fret about the delay and become frustrated trying to determine the reason He does not move quickly on our behalf. But there are times when God is doing an inner work – a work that ultimately will glorify Him and change us. It may not look like it on the outside, but something explosive is taking place on the inside. The good work He has begun in us He will see through to the end. Just give Him time. Stand still and see the salvation of the Lord.

What Do You Do With A Ruined Thing?

After this I will return, and will build again the tabernacle of David, which is fallen down; and I will build again the ruins thereof, and I will set it up: That the residue of men might seek after the Lord, and all the Gentiles, upon whom my name is called, saith the Lord, who doeth all these things (Acts 15:16-17).

The word ruin is not neutral. It is a strong word. Typically, when we say something is ruined, we refer to that which is left after something has been destroyed, devastated, or demolished. The word implies that something was once in good condition. It was once serviceable, valuable, and useful. It was once profitable. It was once innocent, pure, and beautiful. Something was once healthy, well, wholesome, robust, fine and fit, hearty and strong.

Now, not every thing that is in a bad condition is something that was ruined. The word ruined implies that something was at some point in its history in good condition. Some things that look bad have been bad all along. Some things are not ruined. They have simply gone from bad to worse.

When people use the word ruined, it is usually a very serious matter. "I lost in the stock market; I am financially ruined." "I committed adultery; my marriage is ruined." "I stole from my company; my reputation is ruined." "I haven't been getting enough rest, sleep, or exercise, and now the doctor says my health is ruined." "My parents died when I was very young; I was raised by people who abused me, and now my life is ruined."

There is a finality that seems to accompany the

word ruined. It suggests that something is over, the dream unattainable, the goal unreachable, the last chapter written, the door closed, the opportunity gone, the matter concluded. Finished.

If someone really believes that an event, person, or problem has ruined them, the evidence of that belief will be reflected in some way in their thinking, behavior, attitude, choices, outlook, and overall approach to life.

What do you do with a ruined thing?

In certain parts of the world are found the cracked or missing walls, fragmented foundations and the like of famous buildings that once stood as examples of the fine architecture of a particular era. These ancient homes, palaces, arenas, and coliseums may have been great centuries ago, but the only thing left standing now is the remnant of what used to be. We call them the ruins. The ruins stand as a reminder of the past.

There are people who spend a lot of time visiting the ruins. They are sightseers who simply want to look.   These sightseers try to imagine how the structure used to look.   They visit the ruins and then move on to the next one.

Others, called archaeologists, dig up and around the ruins.   These scientists excavate and, based on their findings, reach conclusions about ancient civilizations, cultures, and other matters of historical significance. They search for ruins. That's their job. The archaeologists are paid to study the ruins, after which they write books, give lectures, and conduct seminars about their discoveries.

Then there are those who are responsible for keeping the ruins in a ruined state. They have been given oversight, and their job is to preserve these all too often fragile, unstable structures. The goal is a simple one: make sure nothing is removed, disturbed, or changed in any way.

We too have a choice about the ruined things in our lives. We can simply visit and sightsee at our ruined places. We can repeatedly dig up and around our ruined places, or we may choose to preserve and keep the ruined thing in its painful condition. Thankfully, there is another alternative. We can ask God, the Great Restorer of ruined things, to do a new thing in our lives.

God can look at ruined, demolished, wasted, weak, feeble, ugly, and sickly things and see something He can rebuild, repair, renew, restore, recreate, regenerate, reconstruct, remake, and redeem.

God can restore what others have ruined. He can even renew and remake what you have ruined. God can look at something that is old and see something new. He can look at ashes and see beauty. God can look at something broken down and see it built up.

What will you do with the ruined thing?

If The Lord Is With You

Saul replied, "You are not able to go out against this Philistine and fight him; you are only a boy, and he has been a fighting man from his youth" (1 Samuel 17:33 NIV).

He is only a boy. That was the conclusion that Saul the king reached when David said he would fight the giant Goliath. Goliath's first impression of David was the same as Saul's: *"He looked David over and saw that he was only a boy...."* (1 Samuel 17:42 NIV). Both Saul and Goliath looked at David, and all they saw was a boy. But their perception of David was quite different than one of Saul's servants who said: *"I have seen a son of Jesse of Bethlehem who knows how to play a harp. He is a brave <u>man</u> and a <u>warrior</u>. He speaks well and is a fine-looking <u>man</u>. And the Lord is with him"* (1 Samuel 16:18 NIV, emphasis added). Not once does the servant refer to young David as a boy. He sees a warrior. Even though David had fought wild animals and killed a bear and a lion, he had absolutely no experience in fighting wars. Yet the servant sees him as a courageous man and a *man of war.*

How is it that Saul and Goliath looked at David and saw "only a boy," and the servant looked at David and saw a man and warrior? Why such a difference in what they saw? The servant observed something that Saul and Goliath did not. After declaring that David was a man and a warrior, the servant also concluded: *"The Lord is with him."* When God is with you, it makes all the difference. Alone, David was only a boy, but because the Lord was with him, this spiritually sensitive servant saw a man and a warrior.

There is no comparison between who we are with God and who we are without Him. We may look weak, but if God is with us, His strength is made perfect in us. We may look defeated, but if God is with us, we are more than conquerors. We may look powerless, but if God is with us, we can do all things through Christ who strengthens us. Goliaths still fall by the power of the God who is in, with, and for us.

Life-flight

*The Lord hath heard my supplication; the Lord
will receive my prayer (Psalm 6:9).*

One of the most significant developments in
the rescue industry is the so-called life-flight.
When the need is great, the situation desperate, and
the patient so critical that an ambulance and other
traditional rescue procedures are simply inadequate,
the call is issued for a specially-equipped helicopter
with trained medical personnel to take the patient
to emergency treatment. For example, the life-flight
helicopter is used when there is a car accident,
and the traffic is so heavy and backed up that it

blocks the access of the ambulance to the injured. It is also used when someone with a life-threatening illness is in a hospital that does not have the proper equipment and time is running out. The life-flight helicopter will whisk the patient away to a hospital better able to handle his medical needs.

Prayer is the believer's spiritual life-flight. When our situation is critical, and hindrances, obstructions, and barriers of all kinds block our way, prayer is the vehicle that lifts us and takes us over to the place of safety. While there are some challenges you go through, there are others that God will speedily pick you up and take you over. Prayer enables the believer to soar above the fray, the chaos, and the disturbances. Prayer will life-flight us over what has blocked us, stifled us, detained us, discouraged us, and delayed us. Prayer enables us to fly on eagles' wings to a place of healing and comfort.

Friends are not always available to talk us through. Family may not be able to walk us through. You may feel too weak to press your way through.

Take the life-flight called prayer. Prayer transports the believer to the safe place, the place of healing, the place of refuge, and, indeed, the secret place of the Most High. Why not take flight today? Pray!

Do Not Settle For Less Than God's Best

HANNAH (I)

Elkanah her husband would say to her, "Hannah, why are you weeping? Why don't you eat? Why are you downhearted? Don't I mean more to you than ten sons?" (1 Samuel 1:8 NIV).

Childless, desperate Hannah wanted a son. But wouldn't it be easier to simply go along with her husband Elkanah's suggestion that she accept his love and kindness and then get on with life? Hannah's well-meaning husband did not want to see her in such agony and, therefore, asked her to let their relationship be enough. He was asking her to accept and settle for what she already had.

Settling for something less than God's best is not only short-changing you, but that decision could adversely affect generations to come. Because Hannah was not satisfied with less, she became the mother of Samuel, a great prophet, and a bold man of God. Suppose she had settled for less and simply gave up on having a child. Instead, she persisted and made her requests known to God. God answered her prayer, blessed and honored her because she did not settle for less than God's best.

Today, you may be wrestling with whether to settle for less than what you know is God's will for your life. Remember Hannah's example, and listen for the voice of God telling you to persist and persevere.

It's easy to settle for less when you have waited a long time for the best and you see no sign of its arrival. It's easy to settle for less when those who love and care about you suggest that settling for less is best. It's easy to settle for less when you believe you are not worthy of the best. It's easy to settle for less when less is what you are accustomed to and, seemingly, all you have ever known. It's easy to settle for less when every one around you makes decisions and choices that are less than God's best.

But when you know deep within your spirit that God has something better for you, do not be satisfied with anything other than what He has promised. If God told you not to settle for a sixth grade education, then he will help you find a way to finish high school. If God told you to go to college, start looking at your options. If God said it was His plan for you to become a manager on your job, read material about developing managerial skills. If God told you to start your own business, begin looking for creative ways to raise the necessary capital. If God said He would bring you out of your trouble, stand on that promise. If God said He would heal your body, thank Him for health. If God said He would make the impossible possible, express your gratitude even now.   *If* God said it, He will do it. Do not settle for less than God's best.

The Temptation In Offenses

HANNAH (2)

Hannah was praying in her heart, and her lips were moving but her voice was not heard. Eli thought she was drunk and said to her, "How long will you keep on getting drunk? Get rid of your wine" (1 Samuel 1:13-14 NIV).

Eli was wrong. How devastating it must have been for Hannah who was barren and disheartened to arrive at the house of God and then be misunderstood by the man of God. She was praying, and he accused her of drunkenness. It was difficult enough for Hannah to put up with mocking about her childlessness from her husband's other wife - the wife who had sons and daughters. While painful, the ridicule from her adversary was expected. The condemnation from the priest was not.

When the priest, Eli, misinterpreted her behavior, Hannah could have become offended and decided that was the last straw. Hannah could have bowed her head in despair and concluded that if she could not find comfort at the temple, there was no other place to turn. She could have left the temple angry, hurt, and offended. Oh, how easy it would have been for Hannah to give in to the disappointment and humiliation of being misunderstood, but she did not. Rather, she was honest with the priest, told him she was troubled, and informed him that she was not drunk. Hannah told Eli she was praying because of her sorrow and grief. At that point, Eli spoke these words: *"Go in peace, and may the God of Israel grant you what you have asked of him"* (1 Samuel 1:17 NIV). If Hannah had let the offense drive her away from the temple, she would have missed her blessing.

We must not let offenses keep us from God's best for our lives. Feeling hurt and offended may result in hasty, premature decisions that later have disastrous consequences. Offenses can consume us, embitter us, and defeat us. We need to follow Hannah's example. She corrected the priest, and she was honest about her pain. Eli then responded with warmth, understanding, and the words of comfort she needed to hear. After she heard Eli's prayer for her, she was no longer despondent. To the contrary, Hannah left the temple a new woman and later became a new mother, the mother of Samuel, a judge and one of the great prophet's of God.

Look at what Hannah would have missed if she had given in to anger, rage, worry and discouragement. Sadly, there are many who have lost their way and their mission simply because they allowed an offense to run them away from God's plan for their lives. Yet, it is the very person or incident you are most offended by that may be the bridge God uses to bring tremendous blessings into your life.

Pregnant With Promises
(Worship While You Wait)

HANNAH (3)

Then Eli answered and said, Go in peace: and
the God of Israel grant thee thy petition that
thou hast asked of him. And she said, Let thine
handmaid find grace in thy sight. So the woman
went her way, and did eat, and her countenance
was no more sad. And they rose up in the
morning early, and worshipped before the Lord
(1 Samuel 1:17-19).

Hannah had been tormented by her adversary,
her husband's other wife, because she did

not have children. She was barren, oppressed, and distressed. Hannah prayed and asked God for a son. After Eli the priest realized she was praying, he told her to go in peace *"... and the God of Israel grant thee thy petition that thou hast asked of him"* (I Samuel 1:17). Upon hearing these words, Hannah's countenance changed; she ate, and she was no longer sad. Her situation had not changed, but she had. Hannah's countenance changed, but her circumstances had not. Hannah's face changed, but the facts had not. Hannah's expression changed, but her condition had not. Hannah's look changed, but her womb had not.

Hannah was not carrying a child, but she was pregnant. After she heard the priest's prayer for her, Hannah was pregnant with the promise of God, the power of God, the purpose of God, the provision of God, the blessing of God, and the love of God. And because of *this* pregnancy, she worshipped God.

When faced with the barren places in life, we

must pray until we receive a word from God. Once we receive that word, our countenance too can change even when our circumstances have not. Like Hannah, we can worship as we wait.

Eventually, Hannah gave birth to Samuel. What does God want to birth in your life? Worship and wait in expectation that what God has promised, He will certainly deliver.

Do You Want An Answer
Or Do You Want A Solution?

*When Jesus saw him lying there and learned
that he had been in this condition for a long time,
he asked him, "Do you want to get well?" "Sir,"
the invalid replied, "I have no one to help me into
the pool when the water is stirred. While I am
trying to get in, someone else goes down ahead
of me." Then Jesus said to him, "Get up! Pick up
your mat and walk" (John 5:6-8 NIV).*

God is more than an answer. He is a solution.
And there is a difference. A solution is always
an answer, but an answer is not always a solution.
Sometimes an answer is just a reply. An answer may

be a response to a question but not necessarily a remedy for a problem. If asked, "Why do you behave the way you do?" the answer may be "Because of my upbringing." Now, that is an answer to the question, but it's not a resolution of the issue at hand.

Centuries ago a story was told about a man described as an invalid for 38 years. He believed he would be healed if someone helped him into a pool when the water was stirred. He mistakenly thought his problem was his inability to reach stirred up water. The man was so fixated on this cure for his illness that when Jesus asked if he wanted to be well, he said, *"I have no one to help me into the pool when the water is stirred"* (John 5:7 NIV). Jesus was trying to direct this man's attention away from the thinking that put him no closer to his healing that day than it did 38 years earlier when he first came to the pool. Jesus commanded him to pick up his mat and walk. The man received his healing after letting go of the 38 year-old stirred water "answer" and obeying Jesus – the Living Water solution.

Could it be that we too are focused on long-held beliefs that get us nowhere? Useless, often paralyzing beliefs keep us stuck in the same place for decades. Many of us believe that our life will only have meaning, peace, and joy when we live in the right community, have the right amount of money, or the right career, or the right person. These beliefs, opinions, and perceptions have not changed anything, but we are so convinced they will, and have rehearsed this thinking for so long, that it blinds us to life-changing solutions.

God wants us to step back, reevaluate, and determine His wisdom, His guidance, and His resolution for our predicament. He can do more than hear the complaint. He can fix the condition. He is the all-wise, all-knowing God. But we must step outside our familiar spiritual box and avail ourselves of the opportunity to hear God's wisdom and His personalized direction. If we take the time to listen, and then obey, the Holy Spirit will direct us to solutions that result in change in our lives - not just for a moment but for a lifetime.

Healing Moments

*And, behold, a woman, which was diseased with
an issue of blood twelve years, came behind him,
and touched the hem of his garment: For she said
within herself, If I may but touch his garment,
I shall be whole. But Jesus turned him about,
and when he saw her, he said, Daughter, be of
good comfort; thy faith hath made thee whole.
And the woman was made whole from that hour
(Matthew 9:20-22).*

Most of us want to experience healing events in
our lives. We want a once-and-for-all cure for
what distresses us, and we want it now. Of course,
there is nothing wrong with healing events. The

Word of God is full of examples of healing events: lepers healed, blind eyes made to see, and deaf ears opened in an instant. There was a woman who bled for 12 years who one day touched the hem of Jesus' garment, and she was immediately healed. This was a healing event. Or so it seems. However, could it be that along her 12-year journey to the *healing event* this woman had *healing moments* – moments that sustained her, moments that encouraged her, moments that made a difference? God uses people to provide healing moments in the lives of others. A kind word to someone in distress, a helping hand to the fallen, a timely "thinking of you card" to the lonely – all of these expressions of love and concern may lead to healing moments for those who are hurting.

Many recall the day, the hour, the very minute they were healed. However, if we look closely and carefully enough, we discover that God allowed the person to have healing moments throughout their life's journey that encouraged, comforted, and strengthened them. The child who was abused at home may have had a teacher who took a special interest in her and found ways to affirm her. That teacher, along with others, provided healing moments that helped sustain the child into adulthood when, hopefully, issues related to the abuse would be addressed.

To be sure, we should appreciate and celebrate that specific time at the altar, that particular prayer that was prayed, that special hour when we knew without a doubt we were healed. But let us also appreciate the moments, those healing moments, God graciously used, and uses, to enable us to survive and move closer to the place of freedom and wholeness in our lives.

Living In The What If
Or The What Now

*Remember ye not the former things, neither
consider the things of old. Behold, I will do a new
thing; now it shall spring forth; shall ye not know
it? I will even make a way in the wilderness, and
rivers in the desert (Isaiah 43:18-19).*

Revisiting and reanalyzing our past choices and mistakes can create quite an internal storm. Typically, the first hint that this storm is brewing begins with "what if?" "What if I had gone to college instead of getting married at such an early age?" "What if I had gone home after the game, as I promised I would, instead of ending up at that party?" "What if I had taken the job with the new company that became such a tremendous success rather than stay with the old job because it was comfortable?" "What if I had married Harry and not Johnny?" "What if I had married Susan and not Sally?" What if? What if? What if? O, the tyranny of the "what ifs?" We can exhaust ourselves looking through life's rear view mirror trying to determine why we went north instead of south, east instead of west, over instead of under, up instead of down.

Berating ourselves about the missed opportunities of the past can also paralyze our future. We fear that our future will also be full of missed opportunities and live in worry and anxiety that we will miss the boat again. "What if I make the wrong decision in the future?" "What if I make the same mistake again and miss out on another opportunity?"

We can choose to fret about the "what if" or we can decide to focus on the "what now?" The "what now" keeps us in the present. It does not look at what happened in the past. It looks at what can be done in the here and now. Focusing on the "what now" does not mean we ignore the mistakes of the past. Rather, we confess and repent of sins, learn from the past, and allow its lessons to benefit us and, through our testimonies, others as well. Obsessing about the "what if" of the past takes away energy better used in determining the "what now." The "what now" implies hope, trust, and belief that there is a God with an answer for the present. The "what now" can be asked in expectation that the God of the here and now is so powerful He can offer more opportunities for us in the present than we have missed in the past. What if or what now? The choice is ours. How reassuring and comforting it is to know that God is doing new things in the lives of His children – even now.

The Perfect Timing Of God

Then the king talked with Gehazi, the servant of the man of God, saying, "Tell me, please, all the great things Elisha has done." Now it happened, as he was telling the king how he had restored the dead to life, that there was the woman whose son he had restored to life, appealing to the king for her house and for her land. And Gehazi said, "My lord, O king, this is the woman, and this is her son whom Elisha restored to life." And when the king asked the woman, she told him. So the king appointed a certain officer for her, saying, "Restore all that was hers, and all the proceeds of the field from the day that she left the land until now" (2 Kings 8:4-6 NKJV).

Coincidence? No. Luck? Absolutely not. A woman who left her homeland for seven years to avoid a famine returned at the absolute perfect time. She had followed the prophet Elisha's instruction to leave her home and her land because of an impending famine. God had her blessing waiting for her return.

When the seven years had passed, she wanted her property back. And the day she decided to ask the king about taking back possession of her home and land, it *just so happened* to be the very day, the very hour, the very moment that someone was telling the king how God used Elisha to bring this same woman's son back from the dead. The king had asked the servant of Elisha, Gehazi, to tell him about Elisha and his many miracles. Gehazi could have told the king about the time Elisha made an axhead float, or the time Elisha poured salt into a spring so the land could produce, or the time Elisha put flour into poisonous stew and people were able to eat without harm. But at the very moment this woman walked in, Gehazi was telling the king how God used Elisha to miraculously restore life to this woman's son, the son she *just happened* to have with her! It's good to keep your testimony nearby. Be ready to tell others of the goodness, the mercy, and the grace of God in your life.

The king was so moved by actually seeing the proof of this miracle, he ordered one of his officers to go with the woman to retrieve her land *and* any income that had been made from her land while she was away those seven years. God gave her back even more than she had when she left.

This woman obeyed God when she gave up her home, and He rewarded her obedience. She knew His voice, followed His leading, and thereby was able to flow into the extraordinary, perfect timing of God.

It just so happened. When we obey God and follow His leading and not our own impulses, we too can have those *just so happened* occurrences in our lives – those unforgettable examples of the divinely appointed, ordained, orchestrated, and perfect timing of an all-knowing God.

Living And Learning

Part II

Apollos

Meanwhile a Jew named Apollos, a native of Alexandria, came to Ephesus. He was a learned man, with a thorough knowledge of the Scriptures. He had been instructed in the way of the Lord, and he spoke with great fervor and taught about Jesus accurately, though he knew only the baptism of John. He began to speak boldly in the synagogue. When Priscilla and Aquila heard him, they invited him to their home and explained to him the way of God more adequately (Acts 18:24-26 NIV).

Brilliant, learned, knowledgeable, fervent, articulate are all accurate descriptions of this man whose name was Apollos. He was a moving, powerful, spellbinding, orator who boldly declared the Scriptures. However, despite his outward polish, his knowledge was limited. Consequently, Priscilla and Aquila took him aside and taught him. After additional instruction, he went on to be a help to other believers. It was also said of Apollos: *"For he vigorously refuted the Jews in public debate, proving from the Scriptures that Jesus was the Christ"* (Acts 18:28 NIV).

While his brilliance, his gift of oratory, and his debating skills are noteworthy, this man's humility and his teachable spirit are most impressive. Apollos could have responded to the invitation for additional instruction from Priscilla and Aquila with arrogance and pride. He could have pointed out to the couple how well the people responded to him. Apollos could have informed them that he did not need their input and that he would learn on his own. Instead, he yielded and graciously submitted to those who knew more than he did. Apollos recognized and accepted the fact that Priscilla and Aquila had more knowledge and more experience. His willingness to receive from the couple increased his effectiveness as a witness for Jesus Christ.

Apollos did not lose his focus. He was clear that his assignment was proclaiming the gospel and not advancing his personal agenda. He pursued souls not fame. The mission was to declare the good news not promote his oratory. Indeed, for Apollos, the message was more important than the messenger. What a lesson for us all.

Listen For The Voice

As I arrived on the outskirts of Damascus about noon, a blinding light blazed out of the skies and I fell to the ground, dazed. I heard a voice: "Saul, Saul, why are you out to get me?" "Who are you, Master?" I asked. He said, "I am Jesus the Nazarene, the One you're hunting down." My companions saw the light, but they didn't hear the conversation (Acts 22:6-9 MSG).

Paul had an amazing experience that revolutionized his life. On his way to persecute believers in Christ, he saw a light and fell to the ground. The end result was that he became a leader in the very movement he was fighting. But Paul did not change because he saw the light. Paul heard a voice. Those around him also saw the light, but they did not hear the conversation.

There are times when we have powerful experiences that we cannot fully explain to those around us. They may even participate to some degree, but as with Paul's companions, others may see the light but not hear the conversation. Paul was illuminated by the voice, not the light. He was enlightened by what he heard, not what he saw. Although it might have made for interesting discussion, the light without the conversation would have meant very little to Paul. Someone may have even come up with an intriguing, plausible scientific explanation for this sudden surge of light, but the dramatic shift in Paul's life came because he heard a voice. This voice gave an instruction: *"He said, 'Get to your feet and enter Damascus. There you'll be told everything that's been set out for you to do'"* (Acts 22:10 MSG). When God gives an assignment, others may not be privy to the conversation. They may observe evidence of something occurring, but the details are for God and the believer. We must not become discouraged when those who only see the light do not understand when our behavior changes in response to a conversation, especially when that conversation is with the Creator who alone gives our life meaning and purpose.

Paul's companions were astonished and awed by the light. But that which God uses to get our attention is not always intended to become the *focus* of our attention. This was not about the light. Learn to look beyond the dramatic and listen for the voice of God. He wants to speak to us. He wants to transform our lives. So don't panic when you, like Paul and his companions, see the unusual and the unexplainable happening in your life. Listen for the voice. He still speaks.

TV - Television Or Theft Of Vision

Glory ye in his holy name: let the heart of them rejoice that seek the LORD. Seek the LORD, and his strength: seek his face evermore (Psalm 105:3-4).

Without question, one of the most powerful and revolutionary inventions is the television. For most of us, it is hard to imagine life without it. While the good that has come from television is immeasurable and simply cannot be questioned, we cannot ignore the very disturbing misuse and abuse of this most wonderful marvel of technology.

Many programs are inspirational, educational, edifying, and uplifting, but far too many are distasteful, insulting, and obscene. However, the problem is not just one of *content*. One nearly universal concern is the amount of *time* children spend vegetating in front of the television. But it is not only the children. Adults also end up flipping from one channel to the next seeking another hour of entertainment, while God waits for us to enter into His presence, tune into Him, and seek His face. Television may end up clouding His version and His vision for our lives. When the time that God wants to spend with us is swallowed up by situation comedy after situation comedy, news broadcast after news broadcast, and reality show after reality show, it is then that television taints and steals our vision.

So, maybe the next time we fast from food, let us also consider turning off the television. While it is almost inconceivable, there actually was a time when the television would "sign off" for the night and resume in the morning.

God should not have to wait until we have exhausted ourselves with channel surfing before He can have an audience with us. Throw away the television? No, that's not necessary; rather, we should monitor the time spent watching it lest we miss the breaking news from God that could radically transform our lives!

Celebrate! Someone Else Received A Blessing!

And it came to pass, that, when Elisabeth heard the salutation of Mary, the babe leaped in her womb; and Elisabeth was filled with the Holy Ghost. And she spake out with a loud voice, and said, Blessed art thou among women, and blessed is the fruit of thy womb (Luke 1:41-42).

Elisabeth and Mary had experienced the miraculous. Although she was beyond childbearing years, God allowed Elisabeth to conceive. Surely, Elisabeth's pregnancy brought her great attention because it was so extraordinary. Yet there was no indication she envied Mary, the virgin, whose pregnancy was even more stunning and improbable. In fact, Elisabeth was humble, excited, and absolutely thrilled that Mary came to visit her. She pointedly took the time to encourage and rejoice over God's mighty work in *Mary's* life.

Unquestionably, there was a difference in their pregnancies because there was a difference in the babies they carried. Elisabeth carried John the Baptist, but Mary carried Jesus the Christ. Elisabeth carried the one who would prepare the way, but Mary carried the one Who was the Way. Elisabeth carried the messenger, but Mary carried the Message. Elisabeth carried the before, while Mary carried the Before and the After, the Alpha and the Omega, the Beginning and the End. Elisabeth carried the one who would decrease, while Mary carried the one Who would increase.

Elisabeth's response to Mary speaks to the importance of receiving the blessings of God without comparing our blessings to others. Appreciate the blessings, the gifts, the talents, that God gives us, and rejoice when God blesses others. We should be humbled when God uses us in any way and excited when He uses others for His cause, His kingdom, and His glory. It really is all about Him.

8/11

So teach us to number our days, that we may apply our hearts unto wisdom (Psalm 90:12).

August 11 is my childhood friend Rita's birthday. Her birthday was only three months before mine, yet Rita took great pleasure in frequently reminding me that she was older. Even now, decades later, I still remember that August 11 is her birthday. But after September 11, 2001, the day that forever changed our country and our world, August 11 took on new meaning. For on August 11, 2001, thousands had about 30 days to live and did not know it. Thousands had entered the season of the last days and did not know it. On August 11, 2001, the clock was ticking, the countdown had begun, zero hour was fast approaching, and their earthly sojourn was near its completion. Very soon their lives would come to a sudden, unexpected, tragic end.

On September 10, 2001, mothers put their babies to bed and tucked them in for the last time but did not know it. Sadly, the next day, the morning of September 11, 2001, husbands and wives kissed for the last time and did not know it. Neighbors greeted each other for the last time and did not know it. Commuters read the newspaper for the last time and did not know it.

What if they had known? Would it have made a difference? More importantly, what would you do if you knew you had entered the last 30 days of your life? Are there relatives to whom you would say, "I love you?" Are there people you would forgive or "I'm sorrys" you would say? Are there hungry people you would feed or sick neighbors you would visit? Are there loved ones, co-workers, or friends you would tell about God's love and His salvation?

Like those who died on 9/11, most of us won't know when we have entered the season of the last days. We won't realize when we have embarked upon the last 30 days of our lives. That's why every day, yes, every moment, should be lived as if it is our last. God, teach us to number our days. Teach us to make the most of this precious gift – the gift of life.

Crooked Healing

*He heals the brokenhearted and binds up their
wounds (Psalm 147:3 NIV).*

Brokenness requires attention of some sort. To
ignore brokenness is to risk disfigurement. A
broken bone left unattended can result in a bone
that heals in a crooked fashion. The pain is not
as intense as it was at the time of injury, but it's
obvious something happened because the bone is
bent, twisted, misshapen, or crooked in some way.

Amateur and professional athletes driven to
succeed will sometimes ignore the pain of broken
bones, and, because of their impatience, short-

circuit the healing process. They may not even allow time for the bone to be set. Consequently, it is not unusual to see an athlete with a crooked finger or toe simply because he rushed back into the sport too soon without allowing ample time for complete healing.

Dealing with emotional brokenness is no different. Many have convinced themselves they have been healed of their emotional brokenness. After ignoring or denying the brokenness for such a long time, they actually believe healing has taken place. But it is a "crooked healing." In reality, the painful feelings have been buried, but they have been buried alive. These emotions, now underground, may actually fuel self-defeating attitudes and decisions, leaving the person puzzled by their inability to stop unwanted, out-of-control behavior. Much like the athlete, these individuals are so eager to get back into the game of life their brokenness is ignored. Or, they do not want to go through the discomfort healing may require. The process needed to address the brokenness is seen as too painful and too long. The result is a "crooked healing." The broken person mistakenly believes they are healthy and functioning well, but when the hurt is denied, others all too often are forced to endure the negative impact of this denial. The "crookedness" is reflected in anger, bitterness, resentment, cynicism, sarcasm, difficulty in relationships, unforgiveness, extreme sensitivity and the like.

Healing may take time, and the pain may not disappear immediately, but it's worth it to go through the process in order to receive a genuine healing. Read God's Word, pray, talk to your pastor, a trusted friend or a counselor. Do what is necessary, take the time, and be open to whatever means God chooses to bring about healing, restoration, and wholeness in your life.

Do You Hear What I Hear?

*When the trumpets sounded, the people shouted,
and at the sound of the trumpet, when the people
gave a loud shout, the wall collapsed; so every
man charged straight in, and they took the city
(Joshua 6:20 NIV).*

Rahab stands out as a great woman of faith.
Although she was a prostitute, she was astute
enough to realize that Israel would destroy her
hometown of Jericho just as Israel had defeated
other nations. Rahab negotiated with two spies from
Israel, and they agreed that if she would hide them,
when Israel came against Jericho, she and all in her

house would be protected. Her only requirement was to hang a scarlet cord from the window.

When Israel marched around Jericho and the walls "came tumbling down," Rahab's trust in the word of the spies put her in a position to hear something very different than the other citizens of Jericho. No doubt the other inhabitants of Jericho were terrified. What a frightful sound it must have been for them. These citizens of Jericho heard the sounds of defeat, but Rahab heard the sound of victory. These citizens heard the sounds of devastation; Rahab heard the sounds of emancipation. They heard the sounds of catastrophe; Rahab heard the sounds of opportunity. They heard the sound of destruction; Rahab heard the sounds of deliverance. They heard the sound of a breaking in; Rahab heard the sound of a breaking out. They heard sounds that struck fear in their hearts; Rahab heard sounds that struck a chord in her spirit. They heard the sounds of mayhem; she heard the sound of music.

When God breaks down Jericho walls around you,

what do you hear? Admittedly, it may be frightening when the seemingly invincible comes down, but for God to come in some things must come down. When that which has insulated you keeps you from receiving what God has for you, that wall must come down. When your wall of protection becomes an obstruction to God's will for your life, that wall must come down. When your source of security actually becomes a stumbling block to your God-ordained future, that wall must come down. For God to move in some situations, it is necessary that some things, some ideas, some habits, and yes, some people, move out. Listen for, even long for, and celebrate Jericho walls coming down in your life. Do you hear what I hear?

The Vessel

But we have this treasure in earthen vessels, that the excellency of the power may be of God, and not of us (2 Corinthians 4:7).

My mother has the proverbial green thumb when it comes to growing African violets. One day I took note of the little, timeworn, discolored, pitcher-like vessel she typically uses to water her violets. It does not look like much; but there are several things that are of interest about this little vessel. (1) It does not become useful until my mother puts her hand on it and picks it up. (2) It cannot pour out until something has been poured in. (3) While faded and marred on the outside, the water on the inside is life-giving. (4) Its job is not done until it is empty.

As with my mother's little green vessel, so it is with those of us who want to be God's vessels. (1) We do not become useful until God puts His hands on us and picks us up out of that which has stagnated us. (2) We cannot pour out to others until the Holy Spirit has been poured into us. Until this happens, we have no power. (3) While we may not appear to be much on the outside, when the Holy Spirit dwells on the inside, He can do great things in and through us, enabling us to be used as God's instruments of life. (4) We are true servants when we have emptied ourselves. When we give to others, God replenishes, restores, and renews us for His service and for His glory.

The Miracles And The Message

Just then a woman who had been subject to bleeding for twelve years came up behind him and touched the edge of his cloak. She said to herself, "If I only touch his cloak, I will be healed." Jesus turned and saw her. "Take heart, daughter," he said, "your faith has healed you." And the woman was healed from that moment (Matthew 9:20-22 NIV).

The miracles of Jesus Christ were astounding to say the least. It must have been staggering to see once blind eyes opened, once lame legs walking, and once dead bodies brought back to life. While the miracles are phenomenal, the message in the miracles is transforming. A man blind from birth given the gift of vision was a sight to see, but to hear that his blindness was not a result of sin, but for the purpose of glorifying God, shifts the significance into a totally different arena. It was extraordinary for a woman who bled for twelve long years to touch the hem of Jesus' garment and be healed; however, the emphasis of the event moves to Jesus' response that her *faith* made her whole.

Seeing and receiving the miraculous can be awe-inspiring, but hearing and heeding the message of the miracle can be revolutionizing. While miracles can stop you in your tracks, the message of the miracle can send your life into a completely new direction.

So let's celebrate the miracles, and let's learn from the message. Indeed, the resurrection of Jesus was like no other miracle. And grace, salvation, and the promise of eternal life are like no other message.

Walking Around Spirituality

For we walk by faith, not by sight (2 Corinthians 5:7).

I treasure the many expressions we Southerners use to paint a picture with our words. For years I heard the saying, "He's smart; he's got good book sense, but he ain't got no common sense." Once I heard a rendition of this old expression that amused me. The essence of it was: "She's smart; she's got good book sense, but she ain't got no 'walking around' sense." For several days I laughed at the expression "ain't got no walking around sense." But then, in the midst of my amusement, a rather sobering thought emerged: It's possible to be "spiritual" but not have any "walking around spirituality."

The more I pondered this not so amusing revelation, the more serious the matter became. To be told that you have book sense but no common sense is an insult typically designed to tell someone who is strong academically that they have done something stupid. The expression suggests the individual is limited because they have intellectual prowess but lack the ability to manage everyday living. It implies that the person does not know how to apply knowledge in any kind of practical fashion.

The same holds true for spiritual matters. It's possible to have a good working knowledge of the content of God's Word, to be smart about religion, but have no "walking around spirituality." There is a world of difference between having religious smarts and applying spirituality to everyday "walking around" living. The person with good "book sense" may graduate Phi Beta Kappa yet irresponsibly create thousands of dollars in credit card debt. Likewise, the religiously smart may recite chapters from the Bible verbatim but not have enough "walking around spirituality" to know that it is prudent to ask God to *"Set a watch, O LORD, before my mouth; keep the door of my lips"* (Psalm 141:3).

"Walking around spirituality" is a practical spirituality in the sense that it addresses the commonplace, the everyday, the "where I live" concerns of life. For example, when a person has a "walking around" faith, it reflects a faith that has walked out of the Sunday school classroom and the sanctuary on Sunday and triumphantly marched onto the job and into the marketplace on Monday.

A "walking around spirituality" is not stagnant. It's not immobilized by adversity. It's not paralyzed by trouble. It's not crippled by struggles. It is not disabled by disappointments. A "walking around spirituality" trusts God, keeps moving and believing no matter the situation or circumstance. It's one thing to know the Word of God, but it is another to walk the Word of God as we sojourn through life.

What Do You Have In The Other Hand?

Trust in the Lord with all thine heart; and lean not unto thine own understanding. In all thy ways acknowledge him, and he shall direct thy paths (Proverbs 3:5-6).

In our country, the months of May and June are filled with excitement, for this is the time of the year when people file into large auditoriums and coliseums in anticipation of THE moment. While parents and friends respectfully listen to the keynote speaker, everyone knows a commencement address is not the focus of this occasion. THE moment occurs when a student walks across a stage, and a principal, professor, or president puts in their hand the certificate, diploma, or degree that symbolizes years of hard work and sacrifice. The student then jubilantly walks back to the seat, with sheepskin in hand, hoping that the paper they hold in their hand will open the door of opportunity to great jobs, positions, and careers. Because of what they hold in their hand, they believe beautiful homes, fine cars, financial success and prosperity are right around the corner. But the question is, "What do they have in the other hand?"

The word commencement is taken from the word commence, which means to start or begin something. Understandably, graduates hold tightly to what they have in their hand because, regardless of their age, it represents new beginnings. But no matter how firmly they grip that degree, as important as it is, there are some life challenges that sheepskin cannot help. That is why it is important to ask, "What do they have in the other hand?" And this is not just a relevant question for graduates. Many have been deceived into believing that an education, a job, a career, a profession, a business, a person, or a particular social status is the key to peace, joy, and contentment. When rejection, divorce, losses, failure, disappointment, crises, and troubles of all kinds come, how disillusioning it is to discover that a degree, job, career, or business is not enough. Regrettably, for far too many, so much emphasis and energy were placed on one hand that "the other hand" is empty.

In "the other hand" we need a relationship with our Creator and a belief in His Word. When we seek and cultivate a relationship with God, it enables us to trust Him and stand on His promises. Taking the inward journey and determining what is really important, it does not take long to discover that when God and His Word are in "the other hand," there is a depth to life that is truly meaningful, rich, and enduring.

Achieve as much as you can. Earn as many

degrees as you desire. Pursue whatever career or business you choose. But frequently ask the question: "What do I have in the other hand?"

The message of Matthew 6:33 is timeless: *"But seek ye first the kingdom of God, and his righteousness; and all these things shall be added unto you."*

Healing Is One Thing, Raising Is Something Else

Then said Martha unto Jesus, Lord, if thou hadst been here, my brother had not died. But I know, that even now, whatsoever thou wilt ask of God, God will give it thee. Jesus saith unto her, Thy brother shall rise again. Martha saith unto him, I know that he shall rise again in the resurrection at the last day. Jesus said unto her, I am the resurrection, and the life: he that believeth in me, though he were dead, yet shall he live (John 11:21-25).

Martha believed Jesus for healing but not for raising. Healing the sick was one thing, raising the dead was something else. Martha expressed her regret that Jesus did not arrive sooner because if He had, she was convinced Jesus would have healed her then sick but now dead brother, Lazarus. Obviously, she had witnessed the Lord's wonder-working, miraculous, healing power at work. However, Martha could not bring herself to believe that the same Jesus who opened eyes closed by blindness could also open eyes closed by death. When He called Lazarus by name, how stunning it was for Martha to see her once dead but now living brother come forth - still in his grave clothes!

How do you limit God? After we have seen God move in certain areas of our lives, we become convinced about His power in *that* area. But God stretches us. He does not want us to limit Him. Just because we have not seen Him do something, does not mean He cannot or that He will not.

Is there something God wants you to believe Him for that is so extraordinary, so off the chart, so incredible, you do not even allow yourself to consider the possibility? If so, remember that with God all things are possible. Just keep on believing, keep dreaming, keep aspiring, keep reaching, keep trusting, and keep expecting. We do not want to ever look back on our lives with regret that we did not fully tap into all that God wants to do in, with, and through us. Don't limit God.

A Stumble May Prevent A Fall

(An old English proverb)

Now unto him who is able to keep you from falling, and to present you faultless before the presence of his glory with exceeding joy, To the only wise God our Saviour, be glory and majesty, dominion and power, both now and ever. Amen (Jude 1:24-25).

M ost of us when walking have every intention to proceed where we are going without incident. There are no plans to stumble, let alone fall, but it can happen if we miss a step and trip up. However, there is a distinct difference between a stumble and a fall. A stumble may allow you to catch yourself while a fall lands you flat on the ground. In our walk with the Lord, we are continuously faced with the potential for both stumbling and falling.

To ignore stumbling is dangerous because life's missteps signal the potential for a fall; and, it is far easier to recover from a stumble than a fall. God can use the stumble to remind us of our vulnerability to falling, which then, hopefully, activates our spiritual antenna and puts us on alert. The stumble may take the form of an ungodly thought that, if not resisted, persists until it poisons our attitude and influences our behavior. Or, it may be an unwise decision with minor repercussions that may lead to more impulsive decisions with horrific consequences.

God is gracious and provides us the opportunity to benefit from our blunders. He is even merciful enough to allow us many stumbles before a fall, but it is up to us to learn from the missteps, the "I almost messed up" choices so that we do not end

up flat on our faces. Thanks be to God who alone
"…is able to keep us from falling" (Jude 1:24).

Drop Your Waterpot

The woman then left her waterpot, and went her way into the city, and saith to the men, Come, see a man, which told me all things that ever I did: is not this the Christ? Then they went out of the city, and came unto him (John 4:28-30).

One of the most riveting and powerful examples of transformation is found in the story commonly known as the woman at the well. This Samaritan woman had five husbands, and the man she was with was not her husband. One day she needed water and came to the well only to discover that a man named Jesus was already there. He talked with her, convicted her, cared for her, and changed her so much so that she dropped her waterpot. After her encounter with Jesus, this woman could have cared less about the water or the pot. Jesus changed her agenda and her life. Her purpose changed. Her focus changed. Her mission changed. She came to the well with a waterpot, but she left with a testimony. She came to the well bound, but she left free. She came to the well with shame, but she left with joy. This woman became a bold witness who told others about Jesus the Christ. The waterpot no longer mattered!

Many have encounters with God, but they try to hold onto their waterpots. They try to hold onto their agendas, their purposes, their projects, their programs, their lifestyles, and their plan for their lives. The waterpot represents the old, the past, and business as usual. God wants to do something new in our lives. God calls us to drop waterpots and take on His mission, His assignment, and His purpose for our lives.

You Have The Right
To Remain Silent

Go, gather together all the Jews that are present in Shushan, and fast ye for me, and neither eat nor drink three days, night or day: I also and my maidens will fast likewise; and so will I go in unto the king, which is not according to the law: and if I perish, I perish (Esther 4:16).

"You have the right to remain silent. Everything you say can and will be held against you in a court of law." Lawyers and legal experts of all kinds recommend that if we are ever in a predicament where these words are spoken, the best thing is to say absolutely nothing. These words indicate someone is in the process of being arrested, and, in the excitement of the moment, if not careful, something might be said that would be used against that person in court. This is an example, like so many others, where silence is a virtue. Truly, silence is golden. There are marriages that might not have ended in divorce if someone knew when to be silent. There are business partnerships that would not have been severed and ended in acrimony if only someone knew when to be silent. There are friends who may never have parted company if only someone had known when to be silent. There are wars that may not have erupted had someone known when to be silent.

However, there are other times when silence is not golden but may lead to confusion and chaos, decimation and devastation, injury and injustice, madness and mayhem, travesty and tragedy, destruction and death.

For centuries, black people were enslaved in

America because too many were too silent for too long. Jews were brutalized and massacred in the Holocaust because too many were too silent for too long. The slaughter of innocents in the Sudan is the result of too many who were too silent for too long.

We can look at the evils around us: senseless murders, substance abuse, gang violence, corrupt politicians, discrimination, racism, and terrorism, and we can fold our hands, turn our backs, and walk into the perceived safety of silence only to discover that silence is not always a safe hiding place. Evil has a way of knocking loudly at the door of even the silent ones.

The argument for maintaining silence seems to be a strong one. "What difference can my one voice make?" "I'm only one person." "One voice cannot make much of a difference." But history disputes this conclusion. There was only one Mahatma Gandhi. There was only one Martin Luther. There was only one Frederick Douglass. There was only one Martin

Luther King, Jr. There was only one Sojourner Truth. There was only one Mary McCloud Bethune. There was only one Mother Teresa.

And there was only one Esther, the queen of a land in which her people had been exiled. When asked to speak to the king on the behalf of her people to prevent the mass slaughter of the Jews, Esther initially chose silence. She was fearful because if she approached the king, and he did not extend his golden scepter, she would die. Mordecai, a member of her family, confronted Esther about her decision. Esther then concluded that silence was no longer an option. Even at the risk of perishing, she courageously spoke up for the Jews. God honored her boldness, and He used her to protect the Jews from genocide.

We, too, may have to choose between silence and speaking up for our God and His cause in our families, with friends, at work, in our communities, and at city hall. Remember Esther. She teaches us that silence is not always a virtue. Silence is not

always golden. When God tells us to speak, silence
is then sin.

That Night The King
Could Not Sleep

That night the king could not sleep. So one was commanded to bring the book of the records of the chronicles; and they were read before the king (Esther 6:1 NKJV).

That night the king could not sleep. The king *could* with a glance summon servants to do his bidding. The king *could* decree and men would live. He *could* speak and men would die. The king *could* command armies to go to war. He was strong! He was mighty! He was grand! He was the king! However, on that night, this powerful, great, and mighty king could not sleep. But this was no ordinary restlessness. This was not a simple case of insomnia. That night sleeplessness was purposely induced by God to set in motion events that would determine the destiny of an honorable man. How amazing the lengths God will go to protect those who honor him.

The events of the next morning would hinge on what took place on that night, the night the king could not sleep. Because he could not sleep, he had someone read from the historical records. God arranged it so the person read about a man named Mordecai who discovered a plot to assassinate the king and, thereby, had saved the king's life. Upon hearing this, the king inquired whether Mordecai had been rewarded for his life-saving deed. He had not.

This is significant and timely because the next morning a prominent government official, Haman, who resented Mordecai for refusing to bow down to him, planned to ask the king to hang Mordicai from gallows that he, Haman, had erected. Much to his surprise, when Haman entered the palace, before he could ask the king to execute Mordecai, the king asked Haman what should be done for a man the king wants to honor. Thinking, in his arrogance, that the king meant him, Haman told the king he would put royal robes on the man, put him on one of the royal horses, and have a special prince parade him through the streets saying this is what happens to the man the king honors. The king thought this was a terrific idea and told Haman to do all of this for Mordecai, and not leave out even one detail! "*So Haman took the robe and the horse, arrayed Mordecai and led him on horseback through the city square, and proclaimed before him, 'Thus shall it be done to the man whom the king delights to honor!'*" (Esther 6:11 NKJV). Haman, Mordecai's enemy, became his valet!

Are you worried about an enemy? Are you concerned about an adversary? Are you being mistreated? Just focus on praying for that person and representing God in the problematic relationship. That is your job. God will always do His.

By the way, later, Haman was hung from the very gallows he prepared for Mordecai, and the king promoted Mordecai to a position of prominence. Thank God, that night the king could not sleep.

Notes

Notes

Notes

Notes

Notes

CPSIA information can be obtained at www.ICGtesting.com
Printed in the USA
236543LV00001B/1/P